I0502635

# Giraffe Coloring Book for Adults

***This book belongs to:***

________________________________

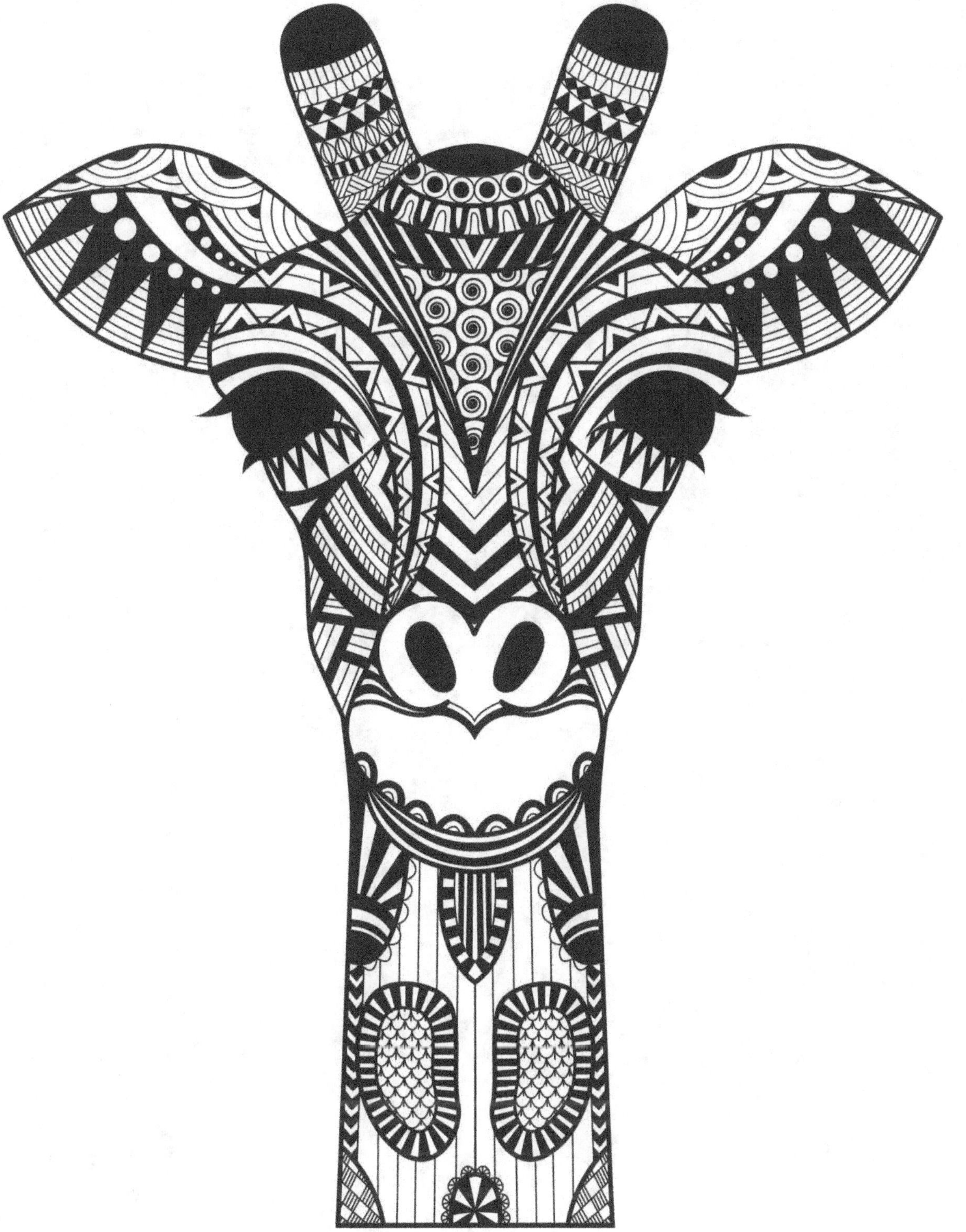

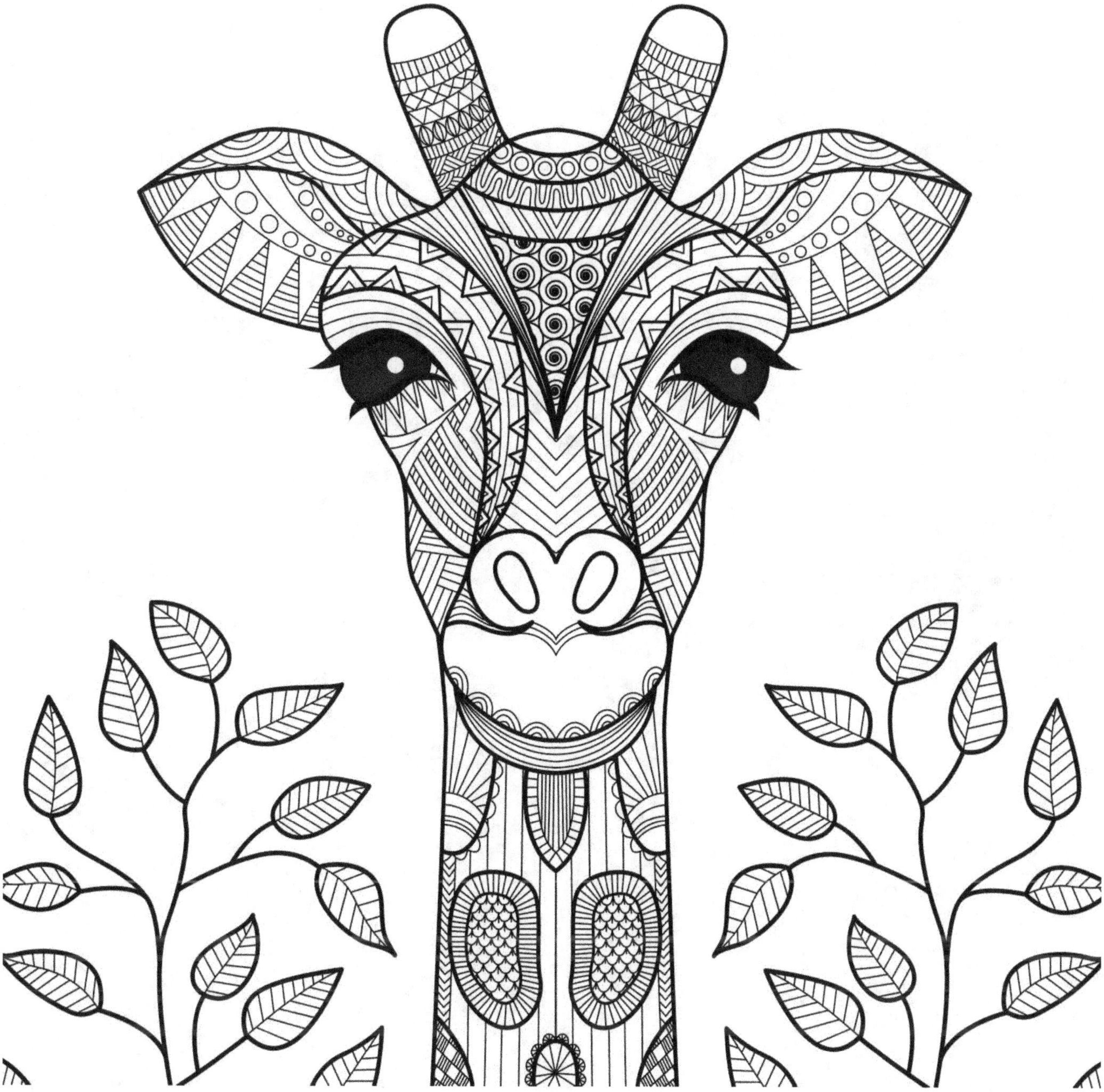

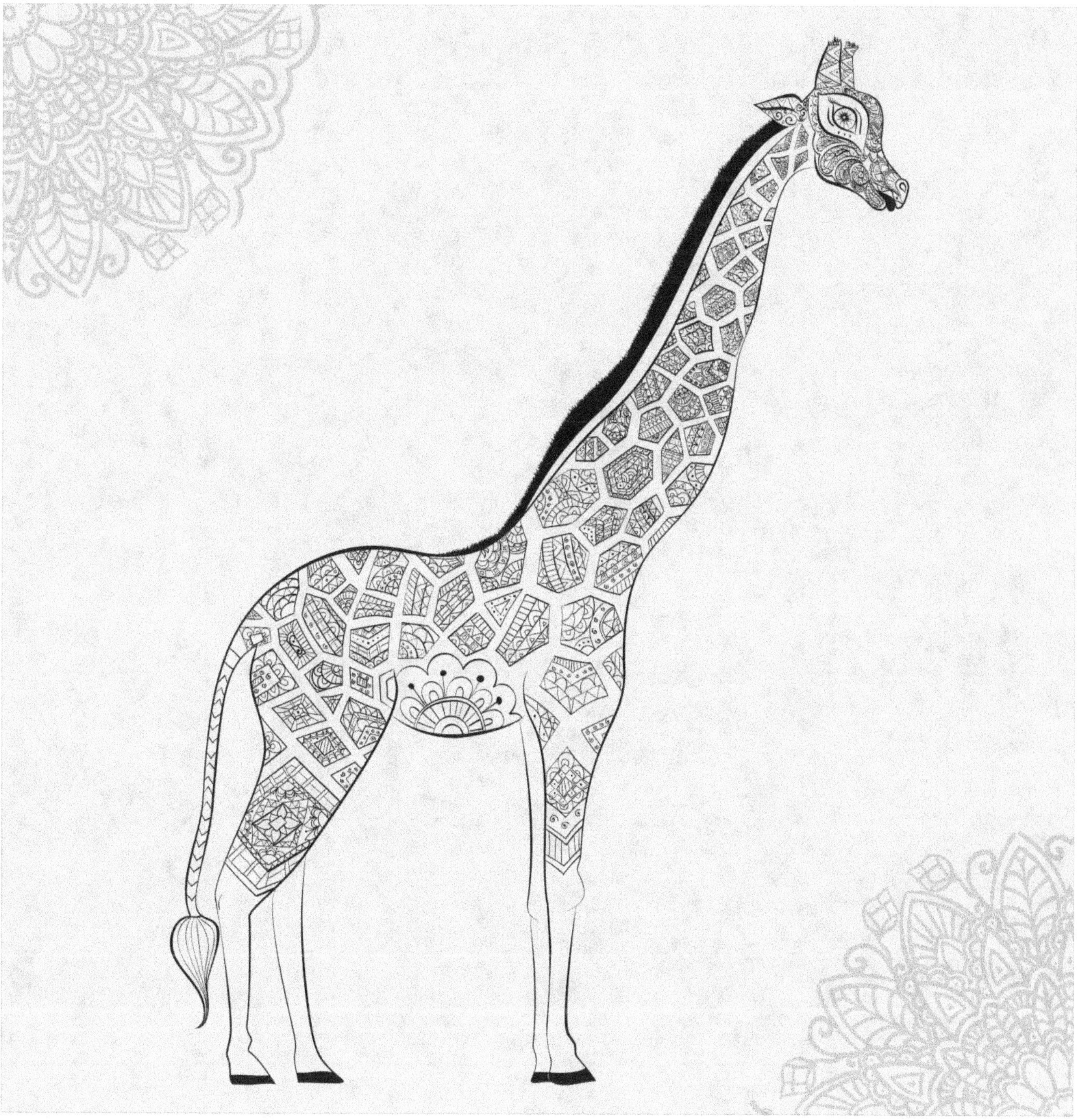

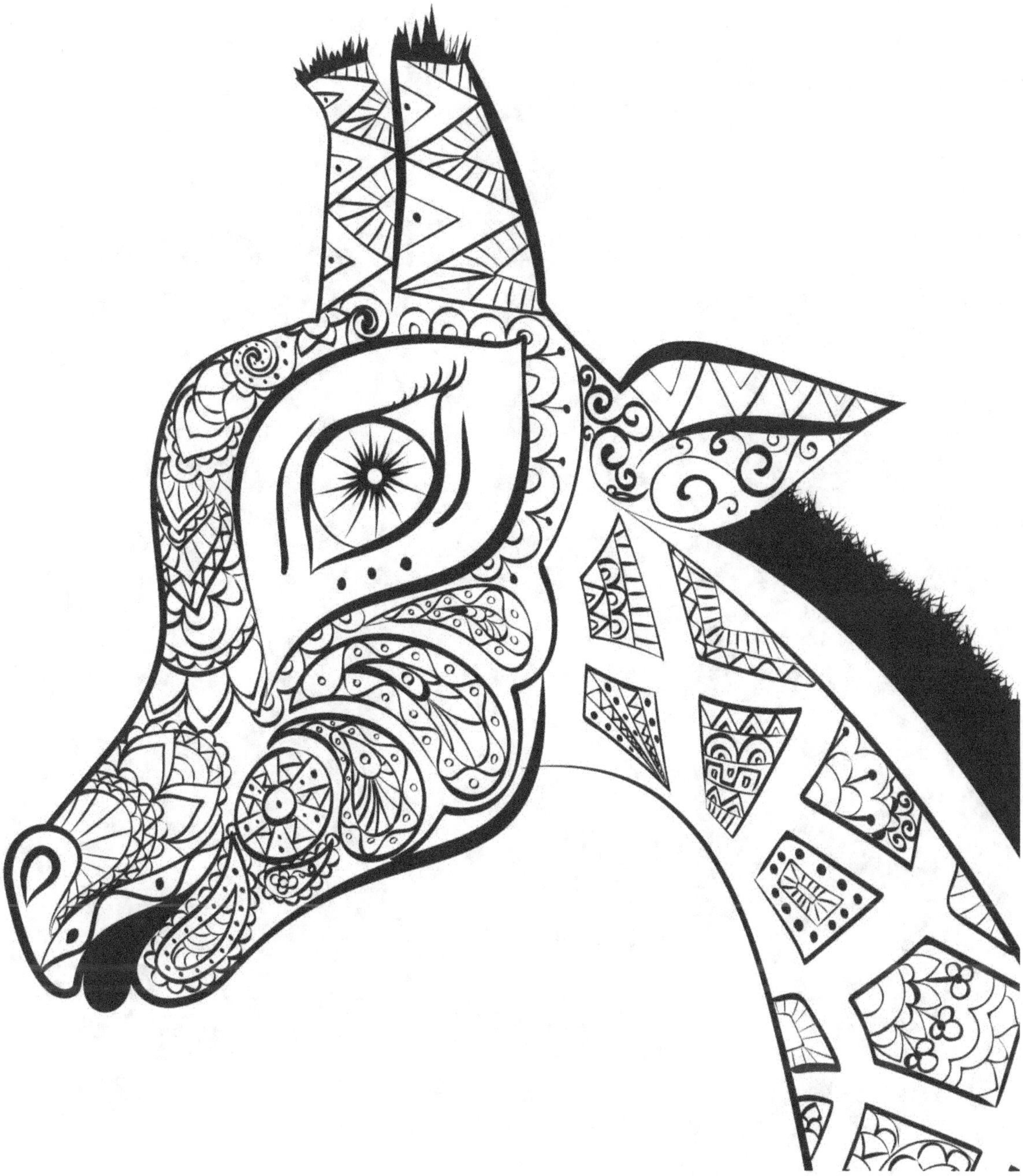

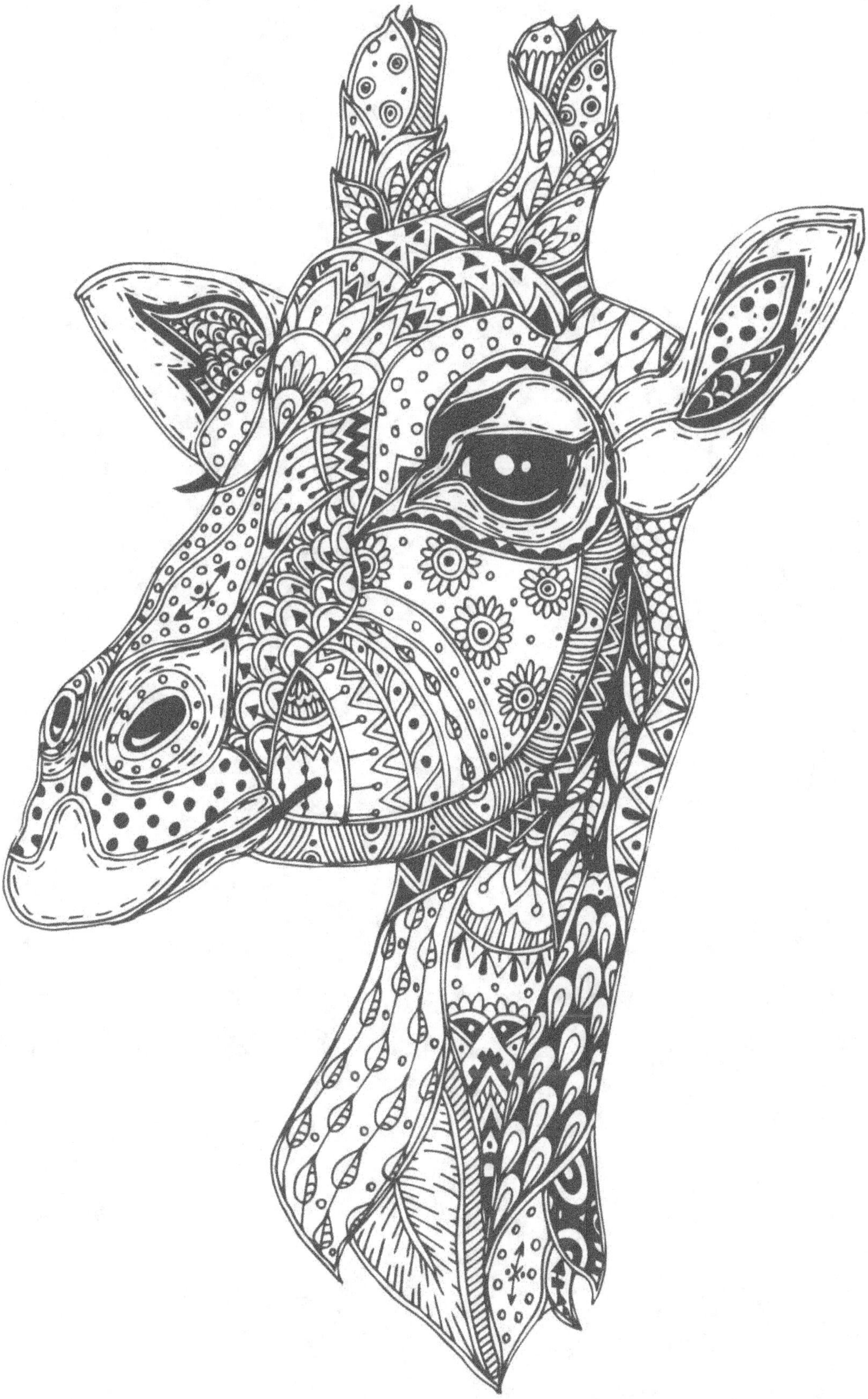

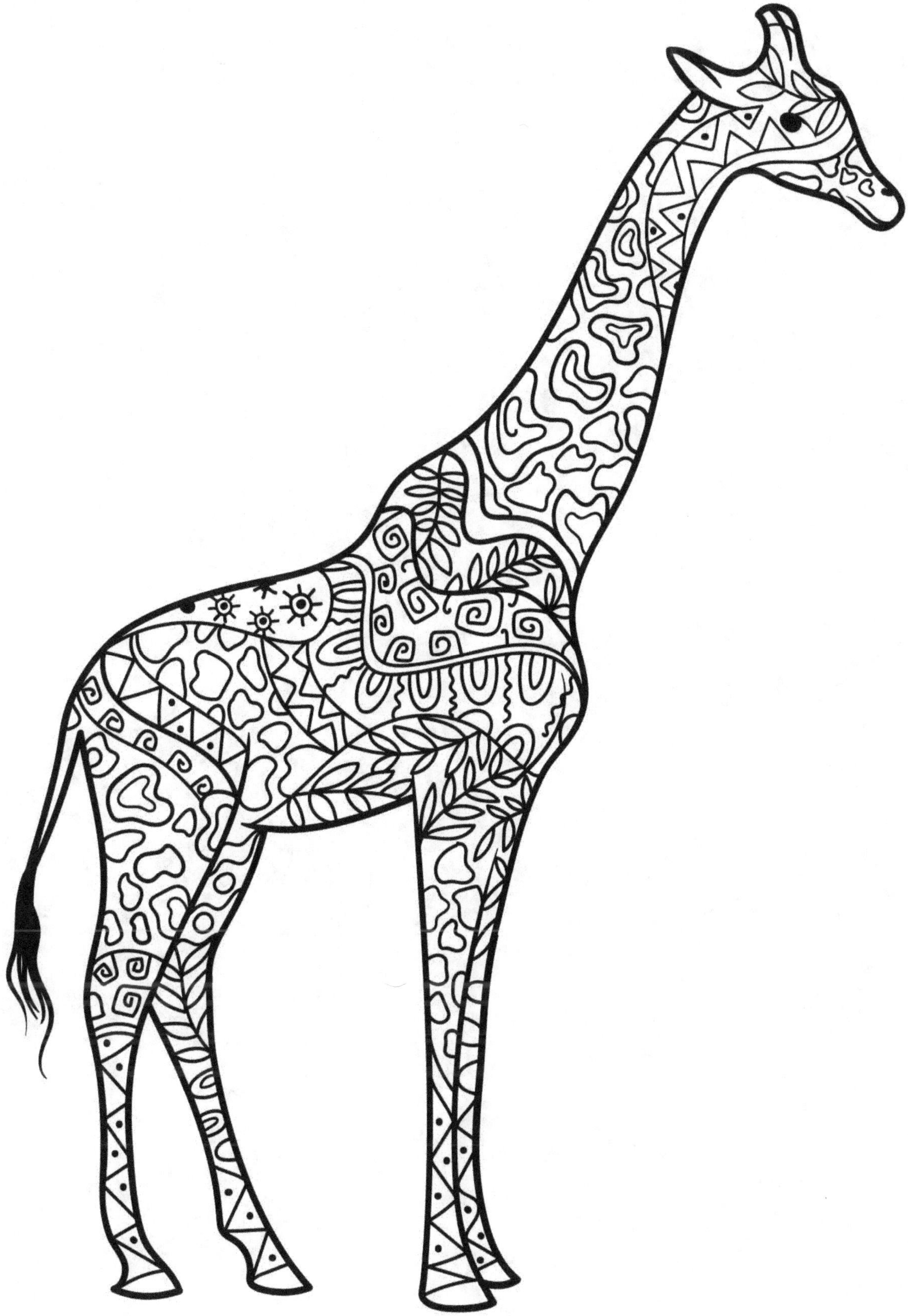

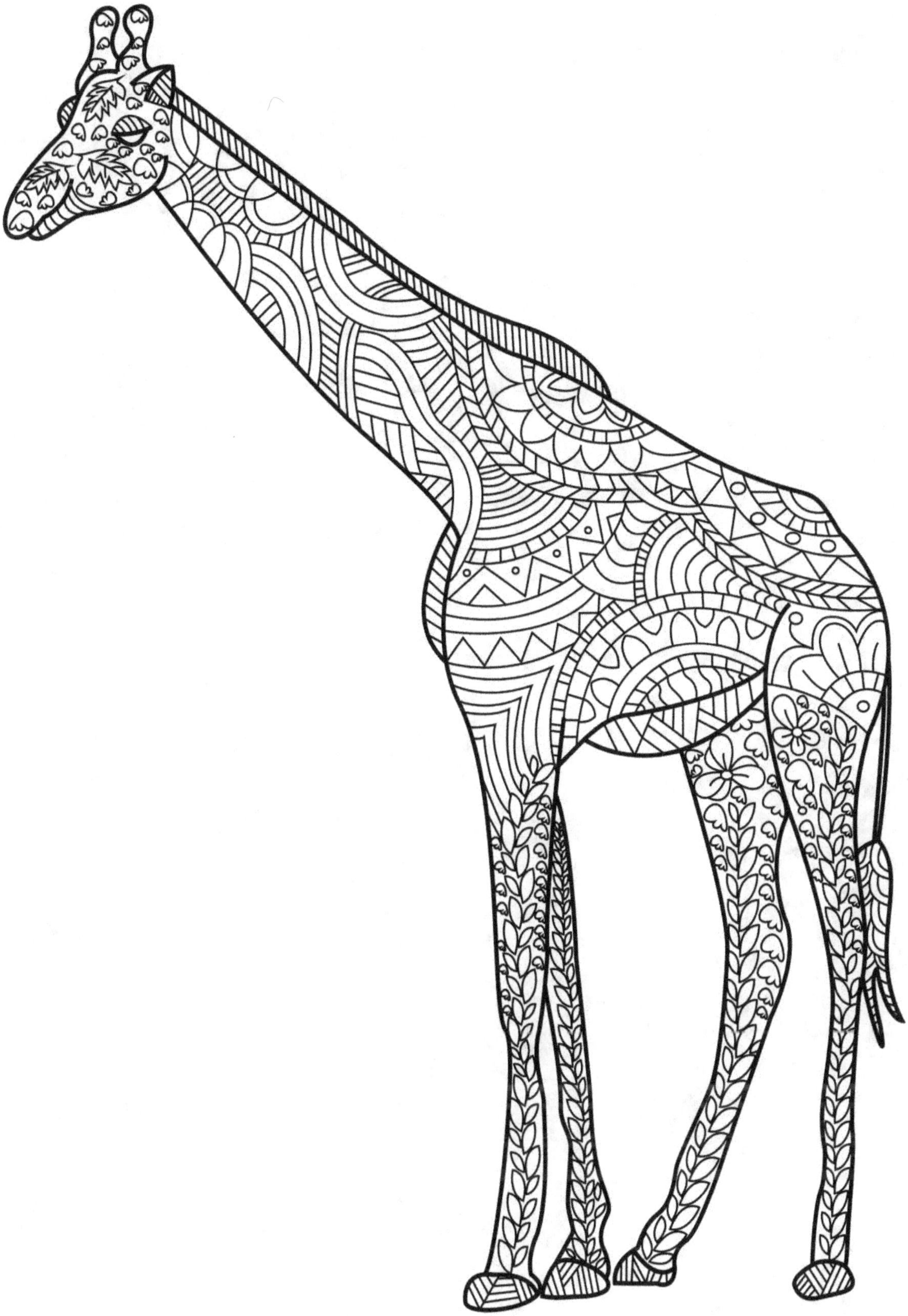

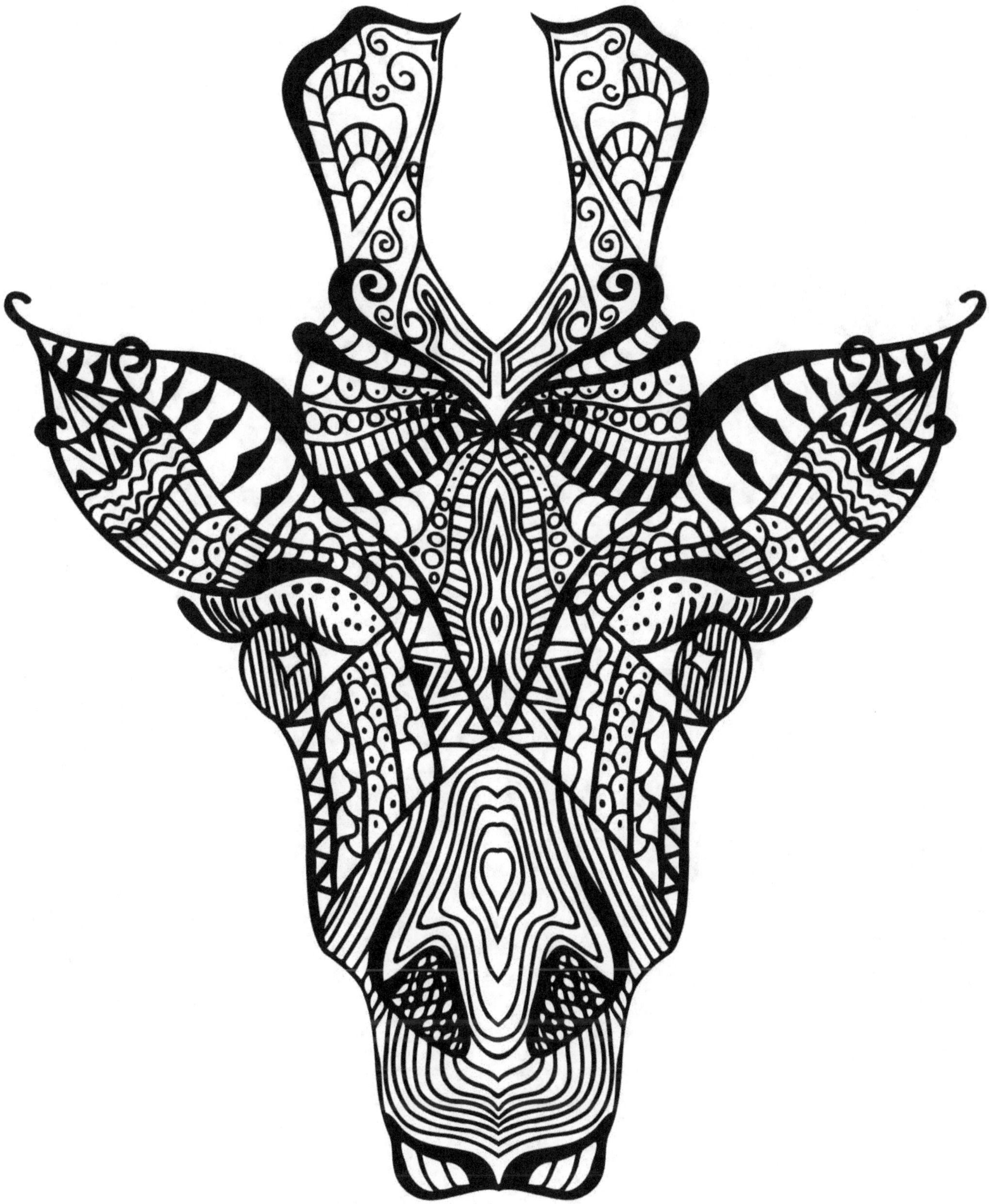

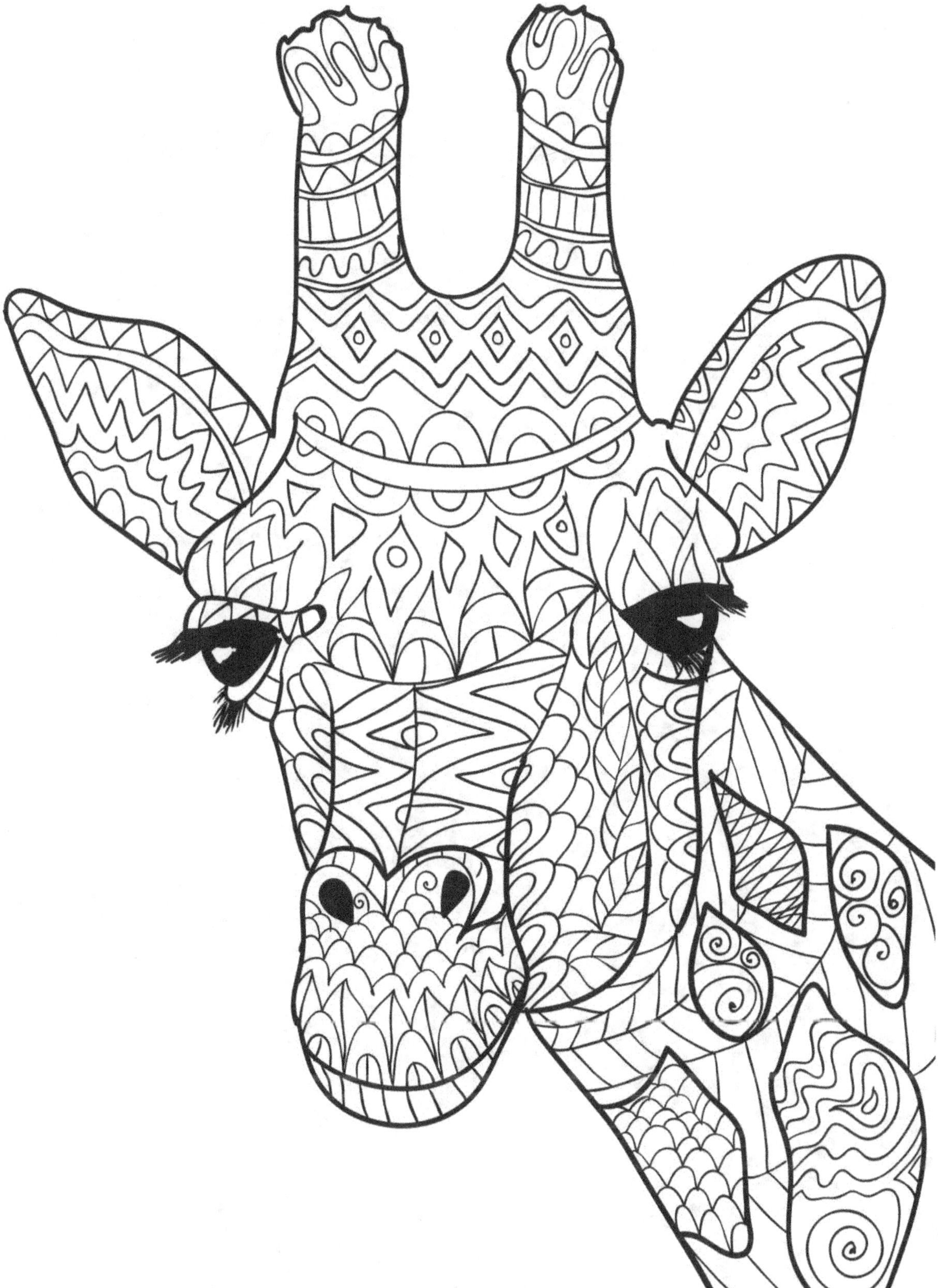

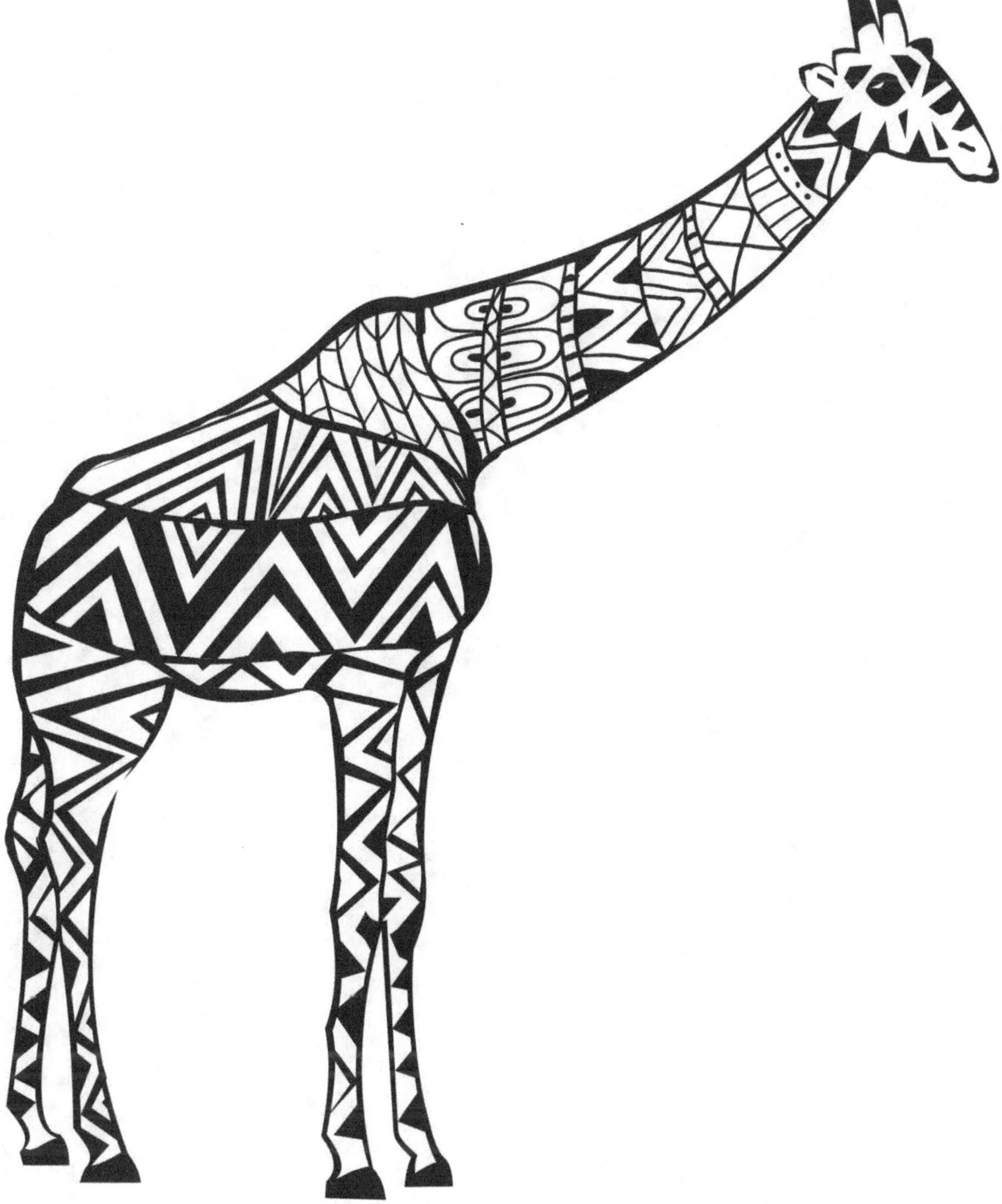

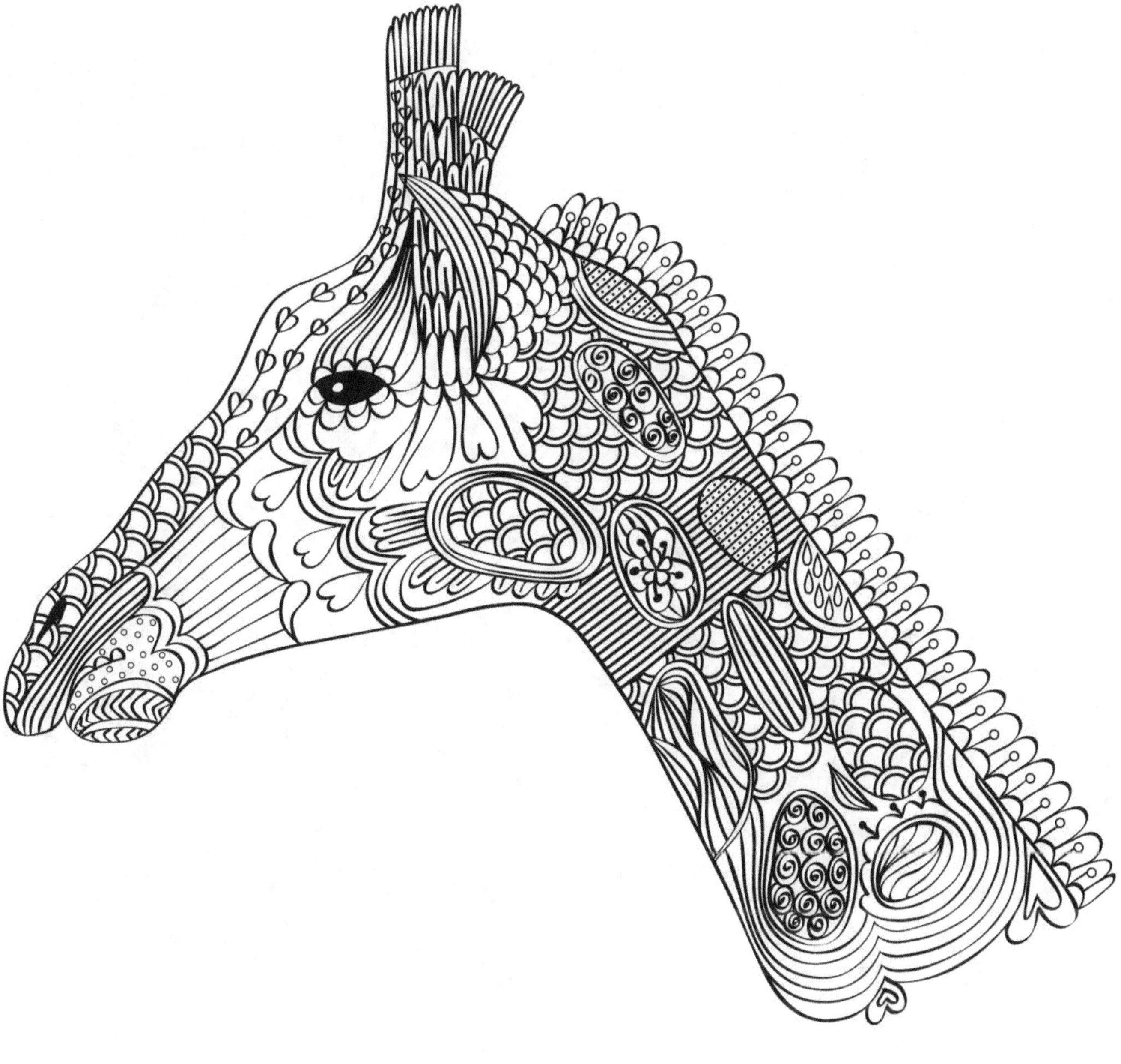

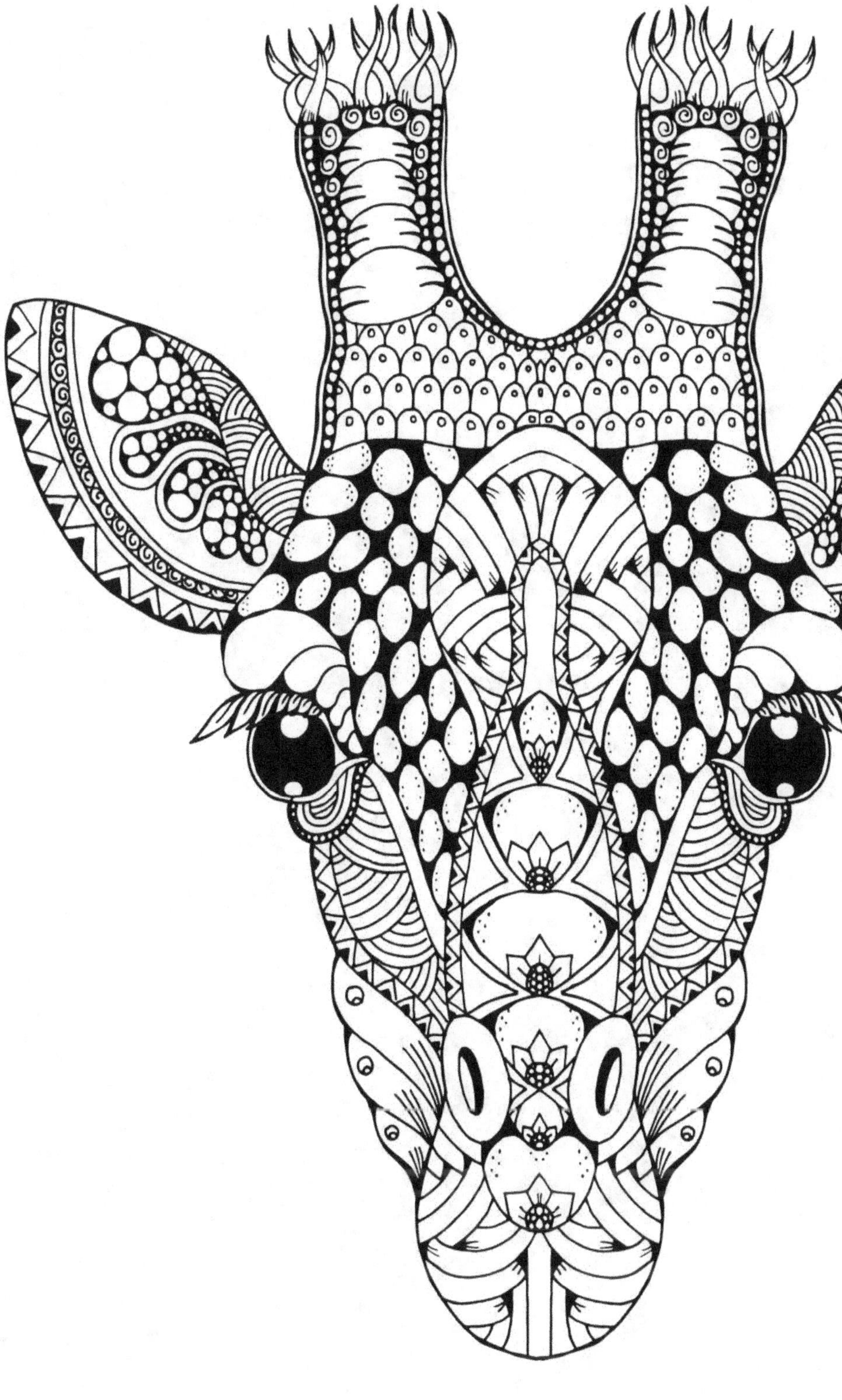

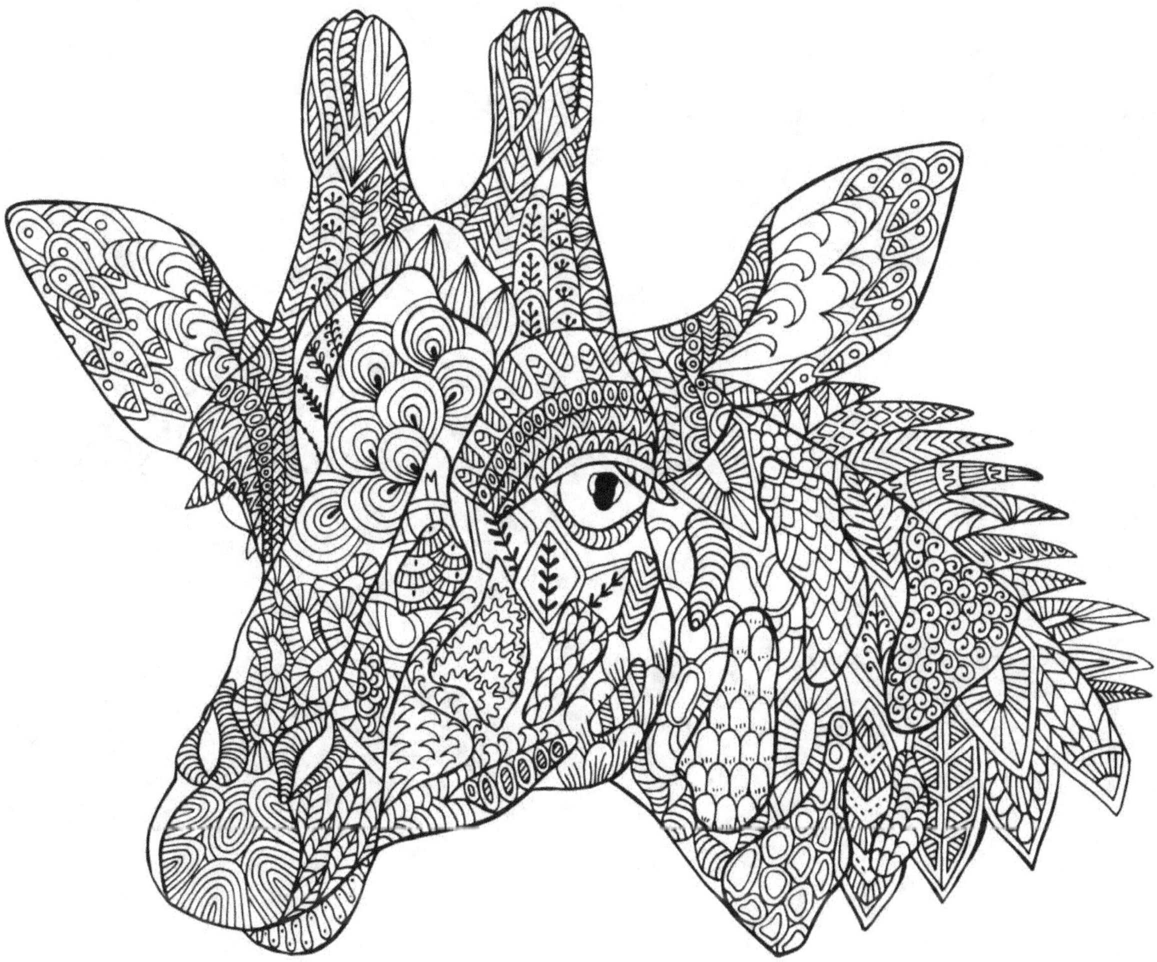

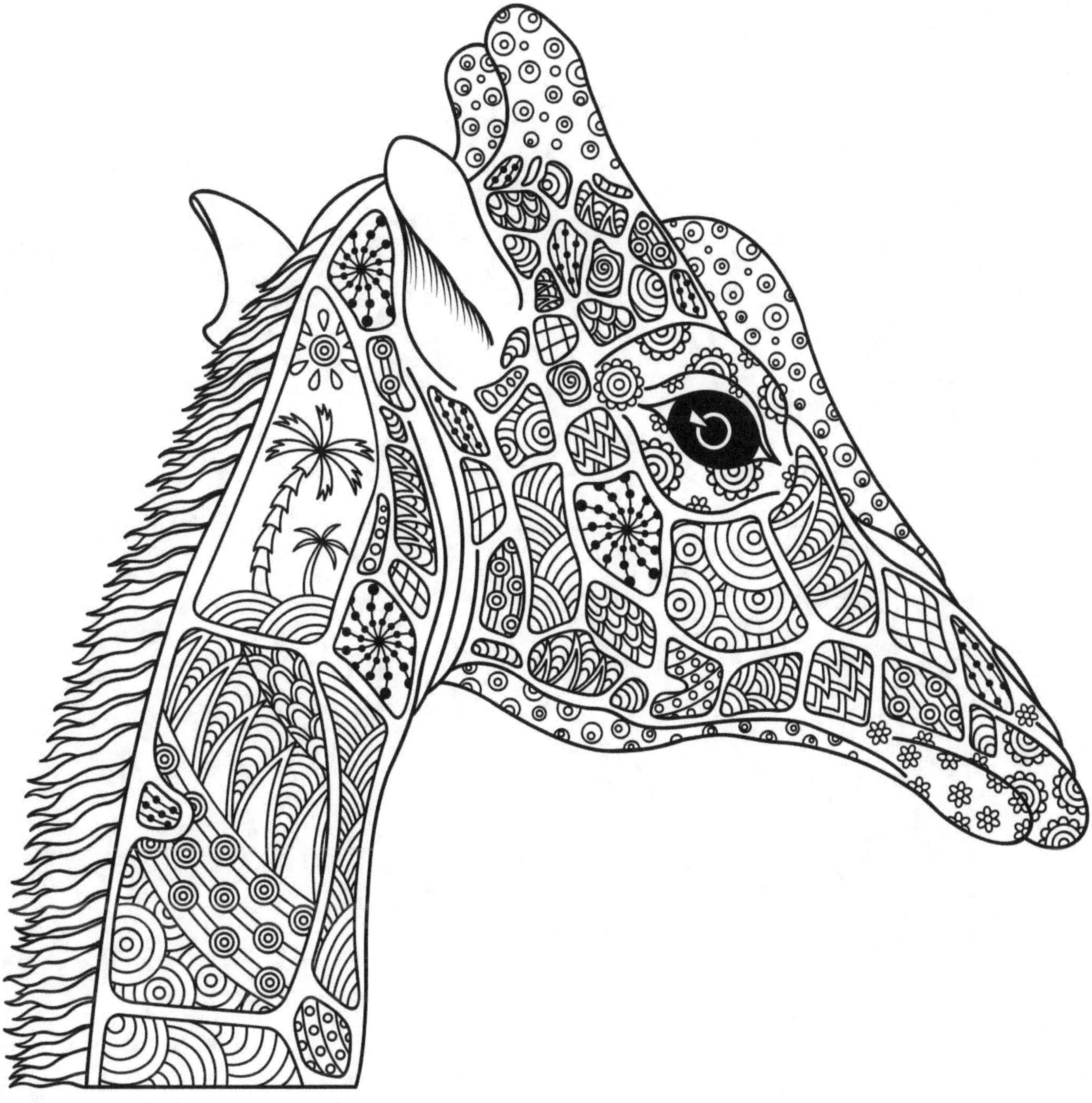

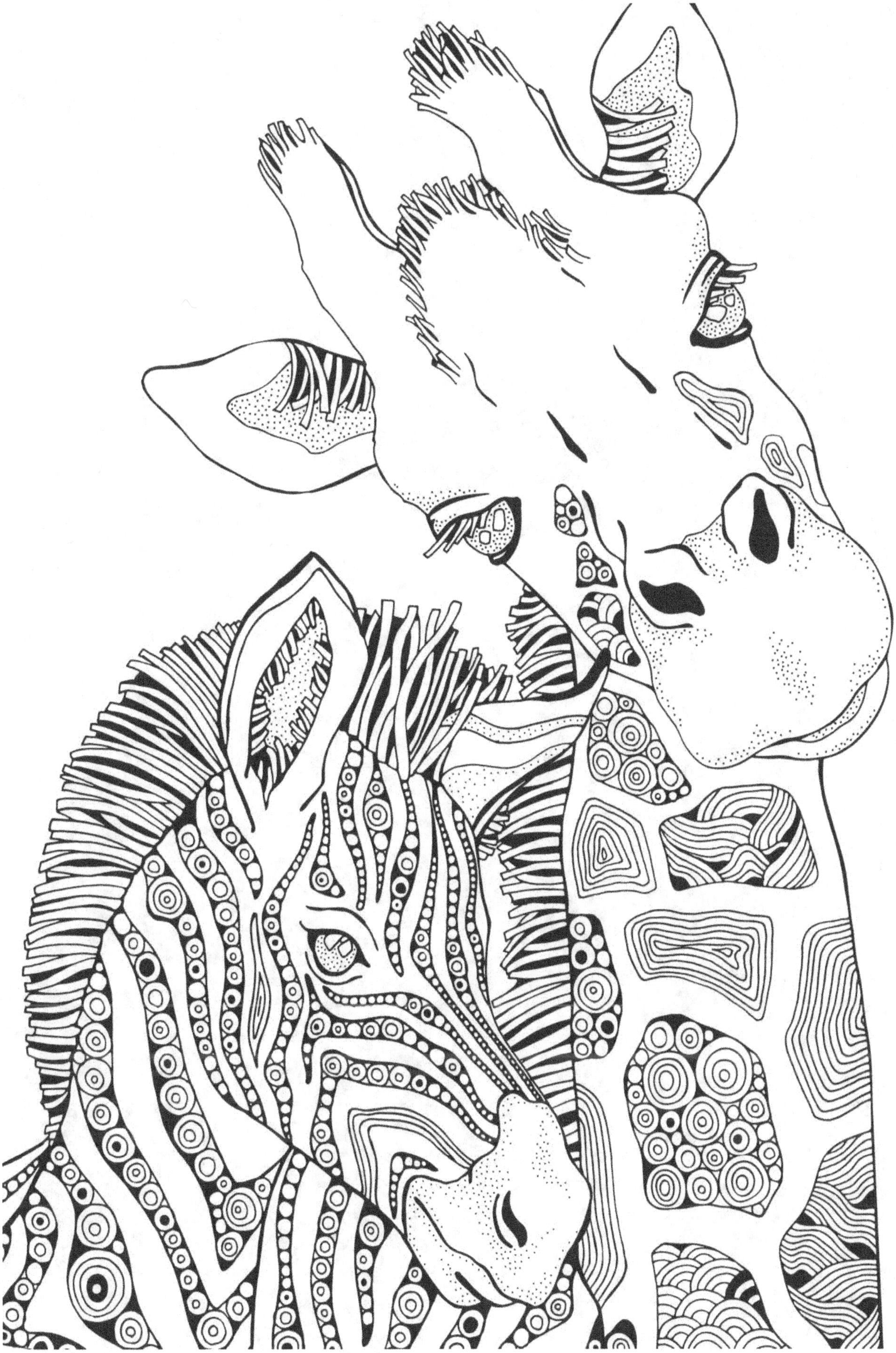

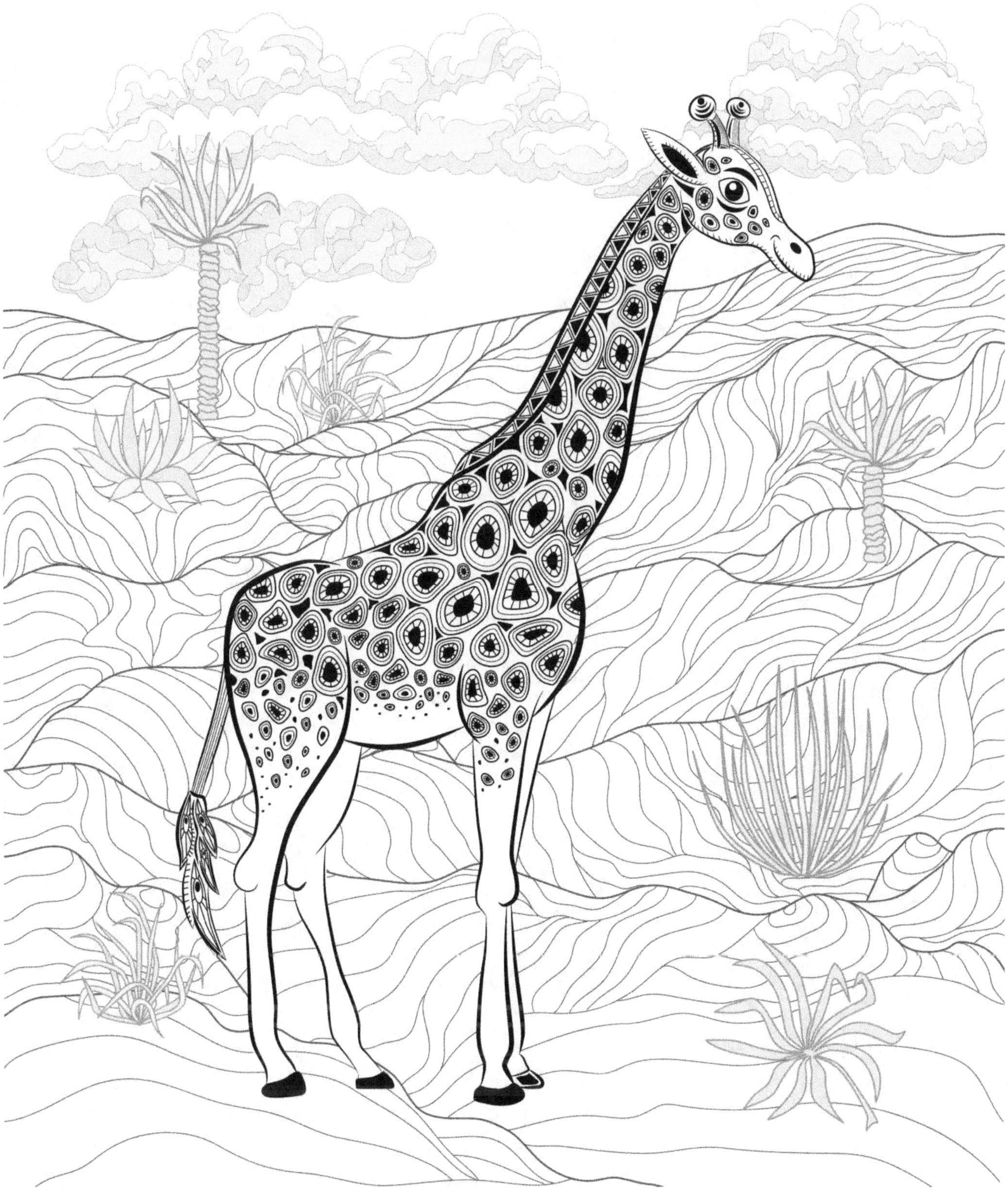

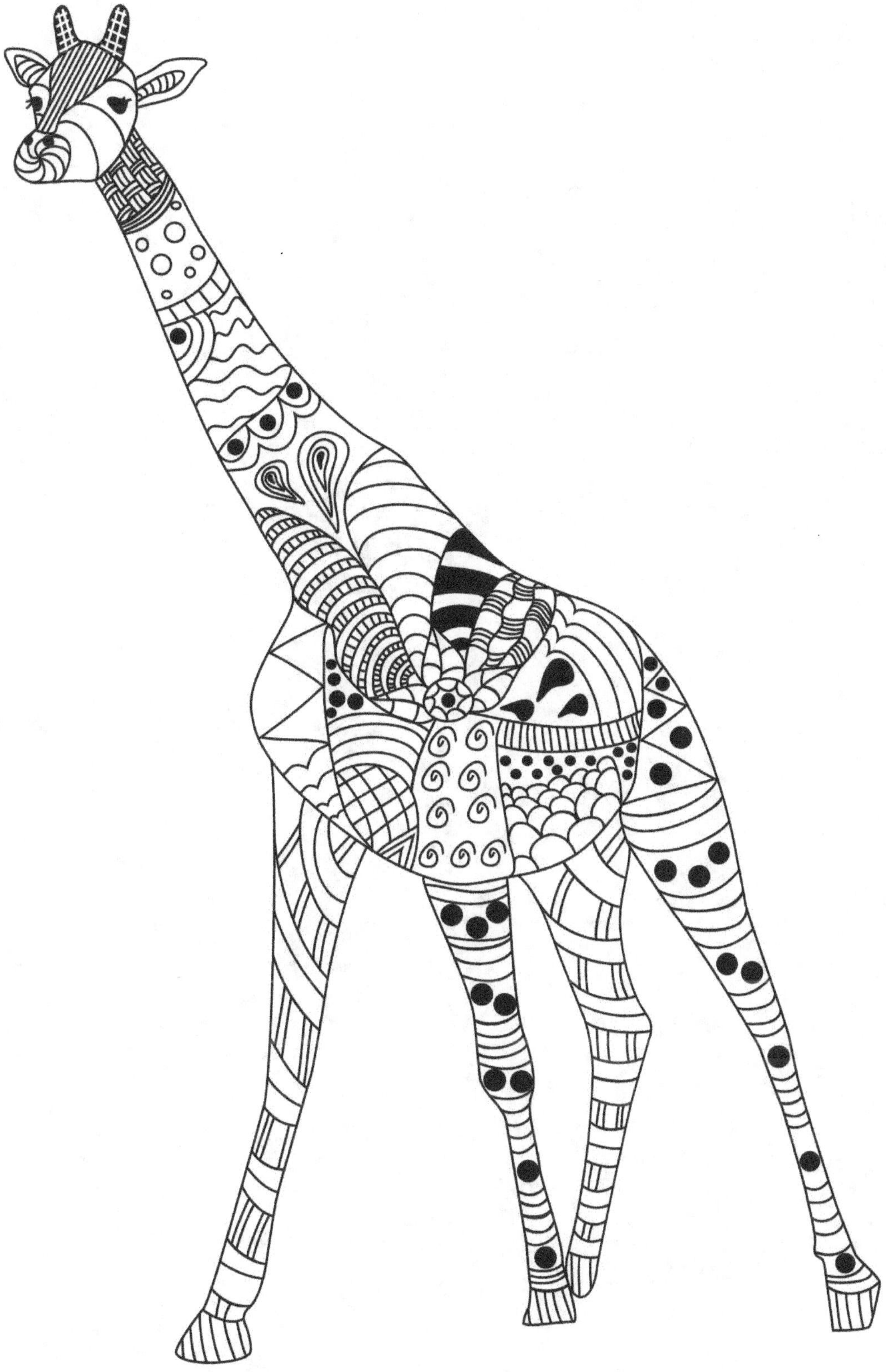

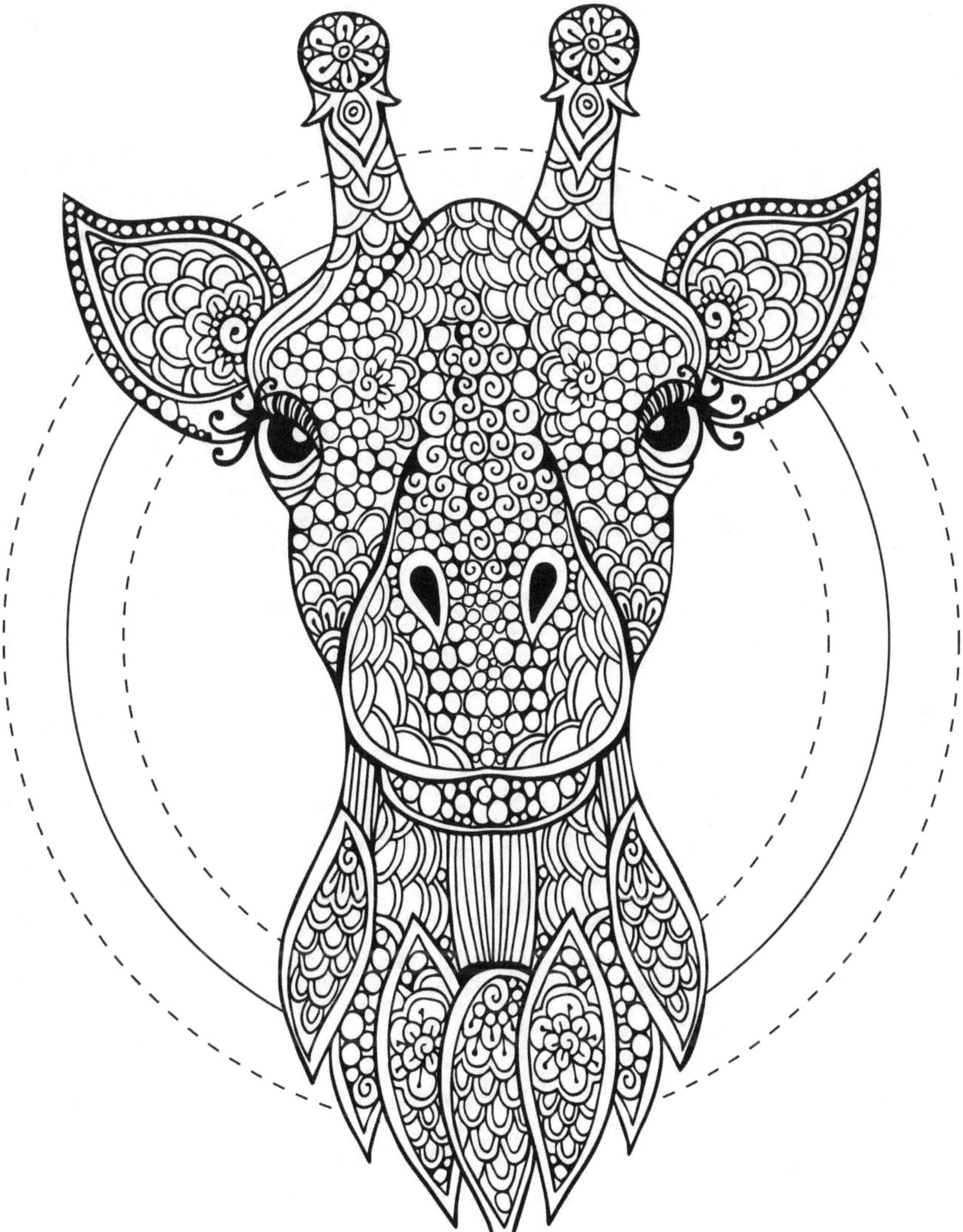

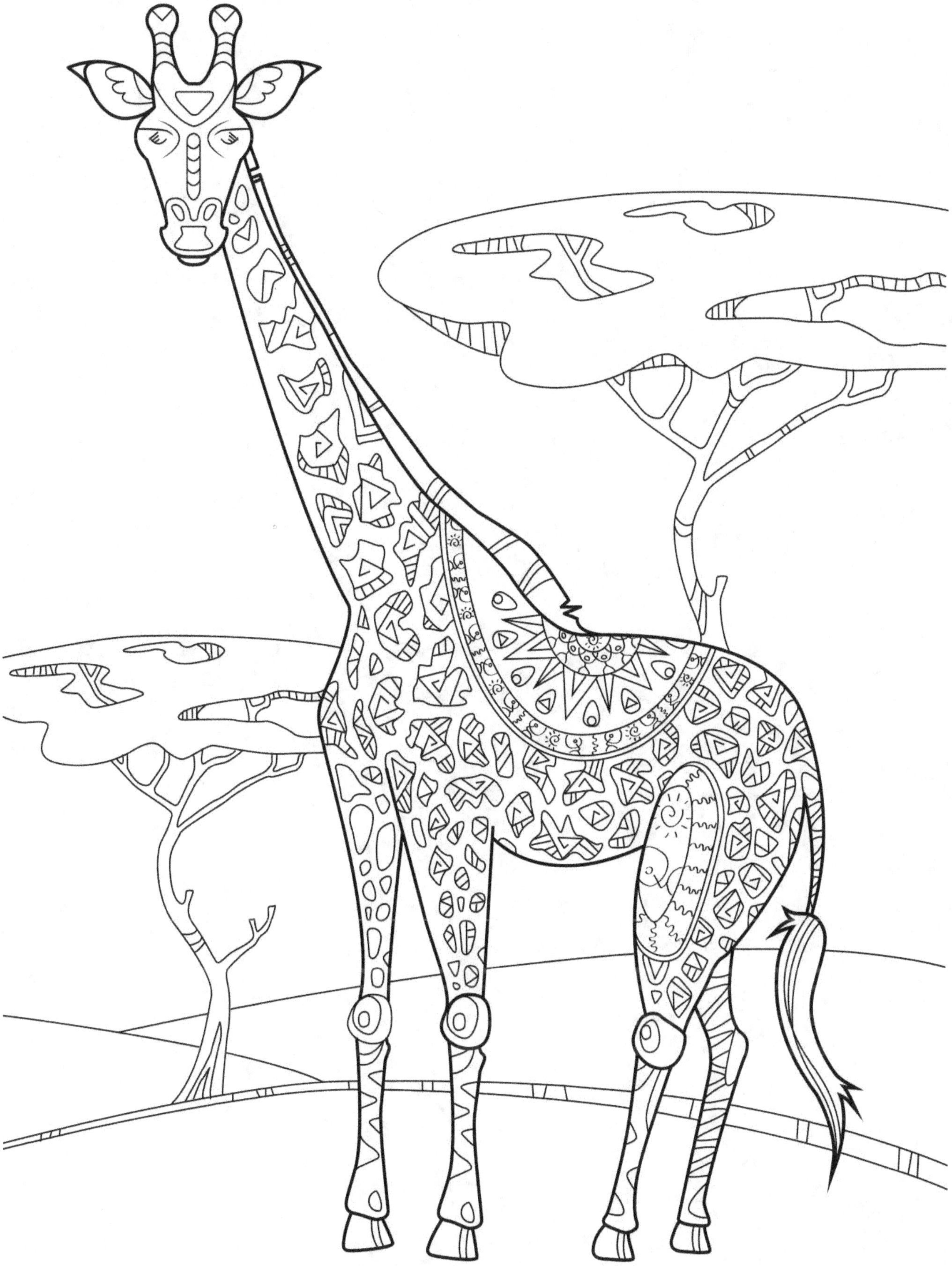

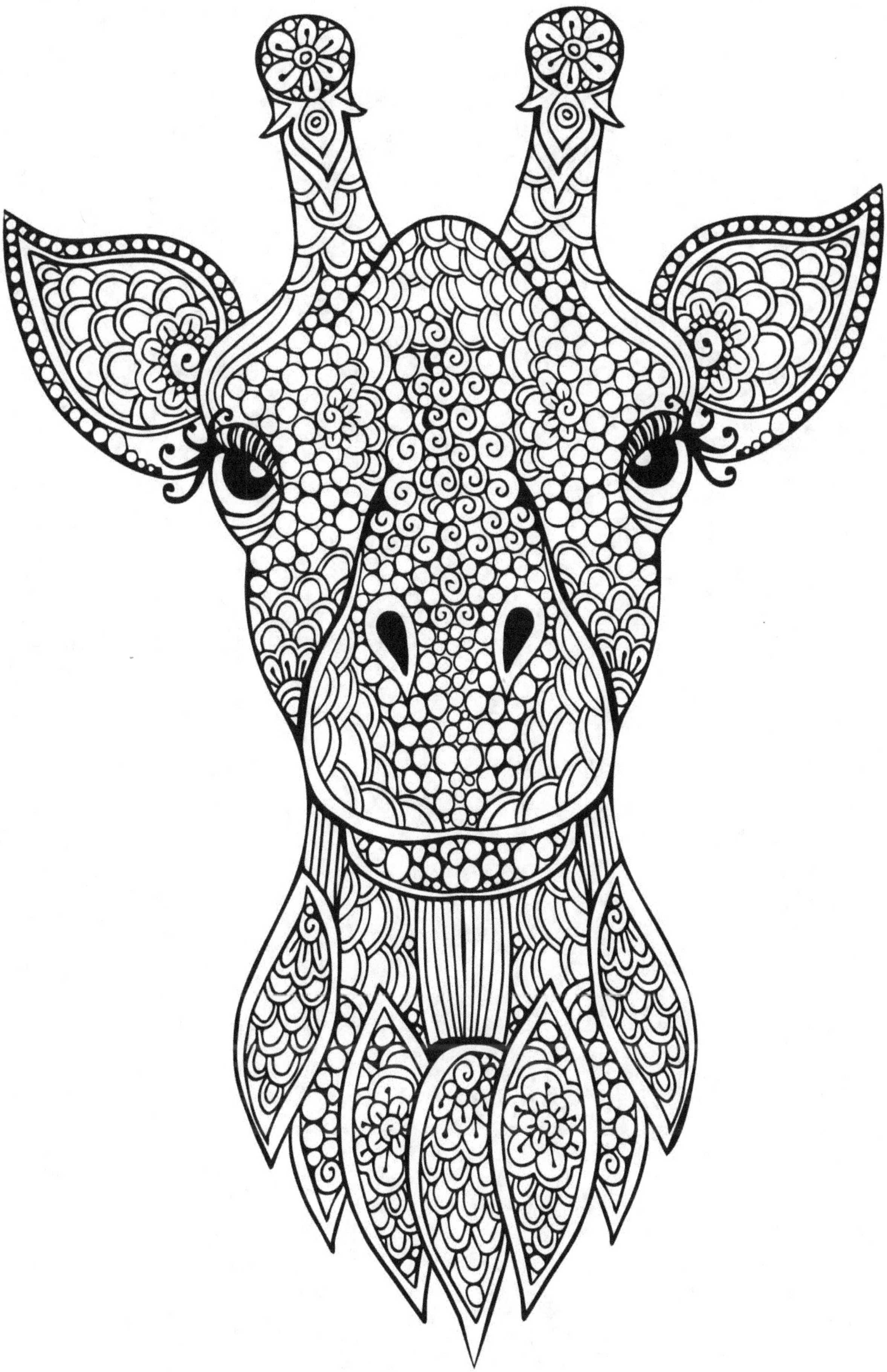

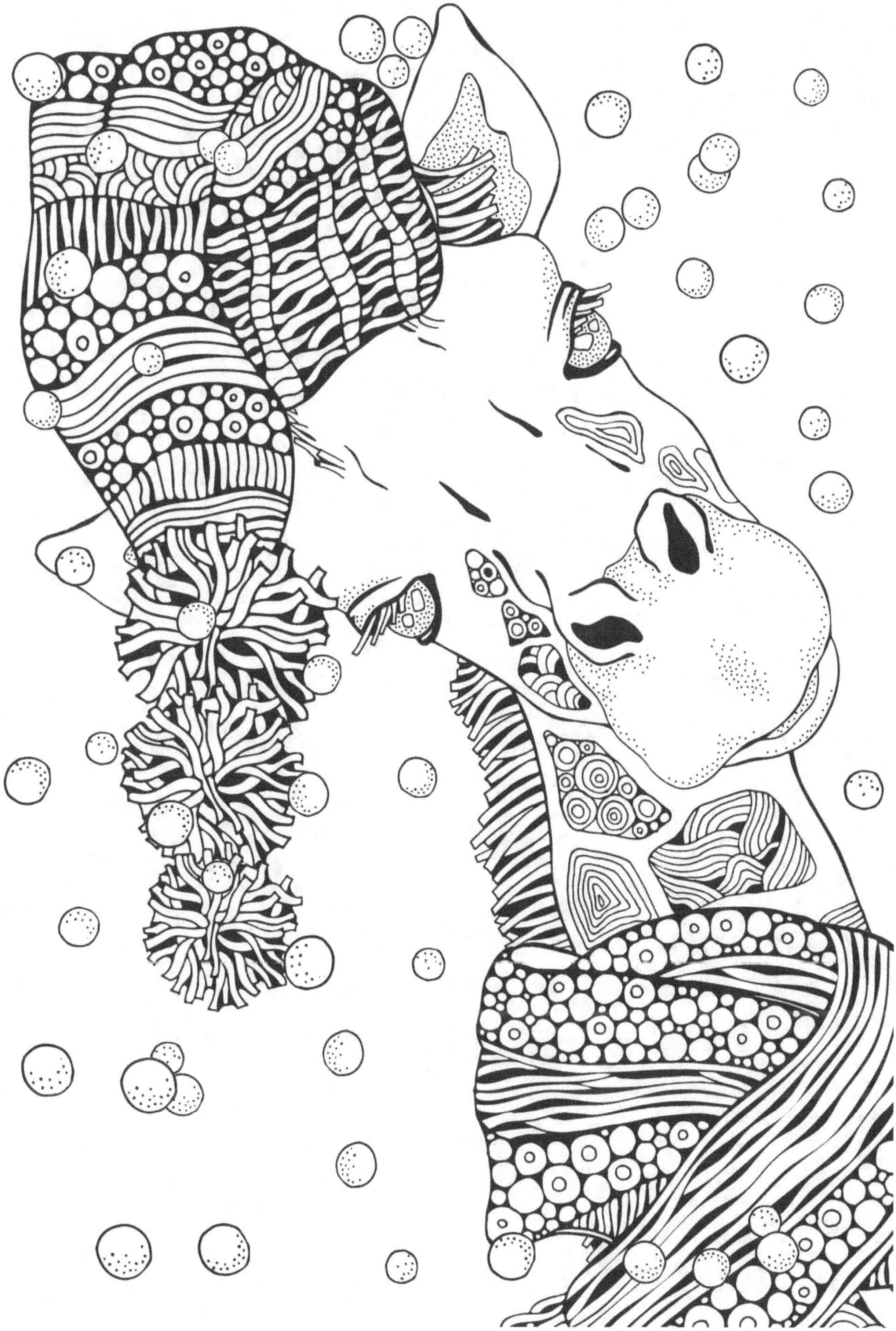

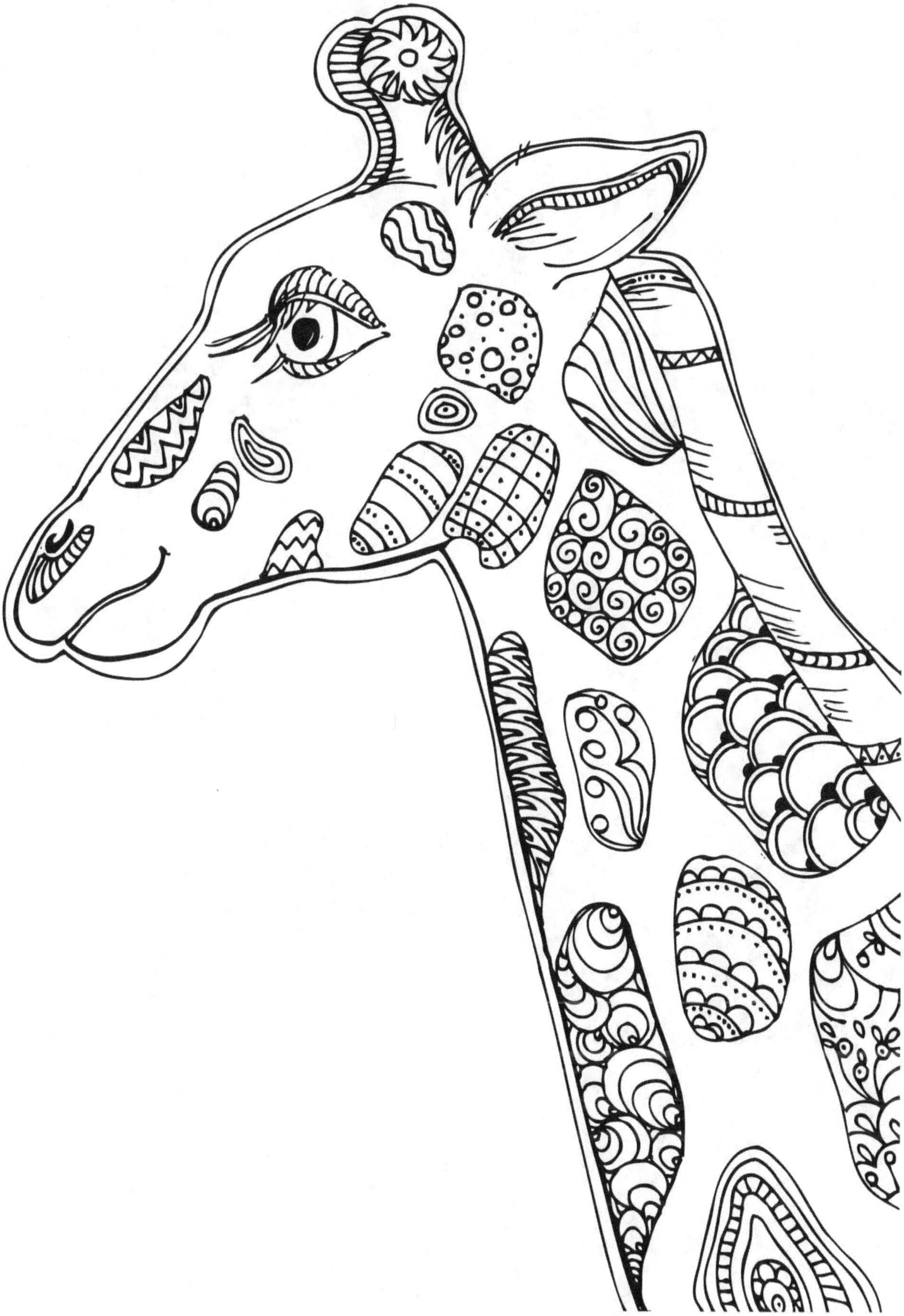

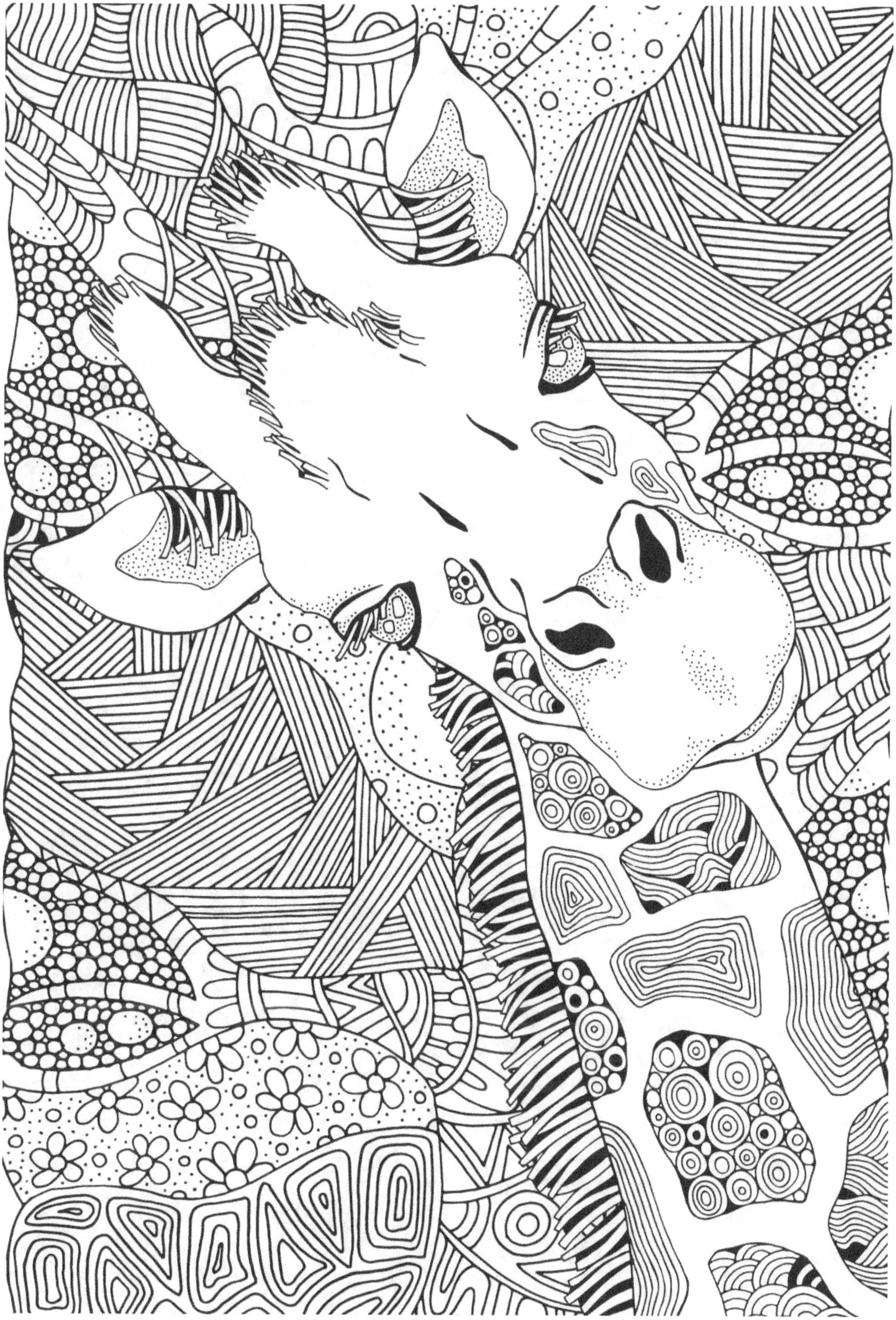

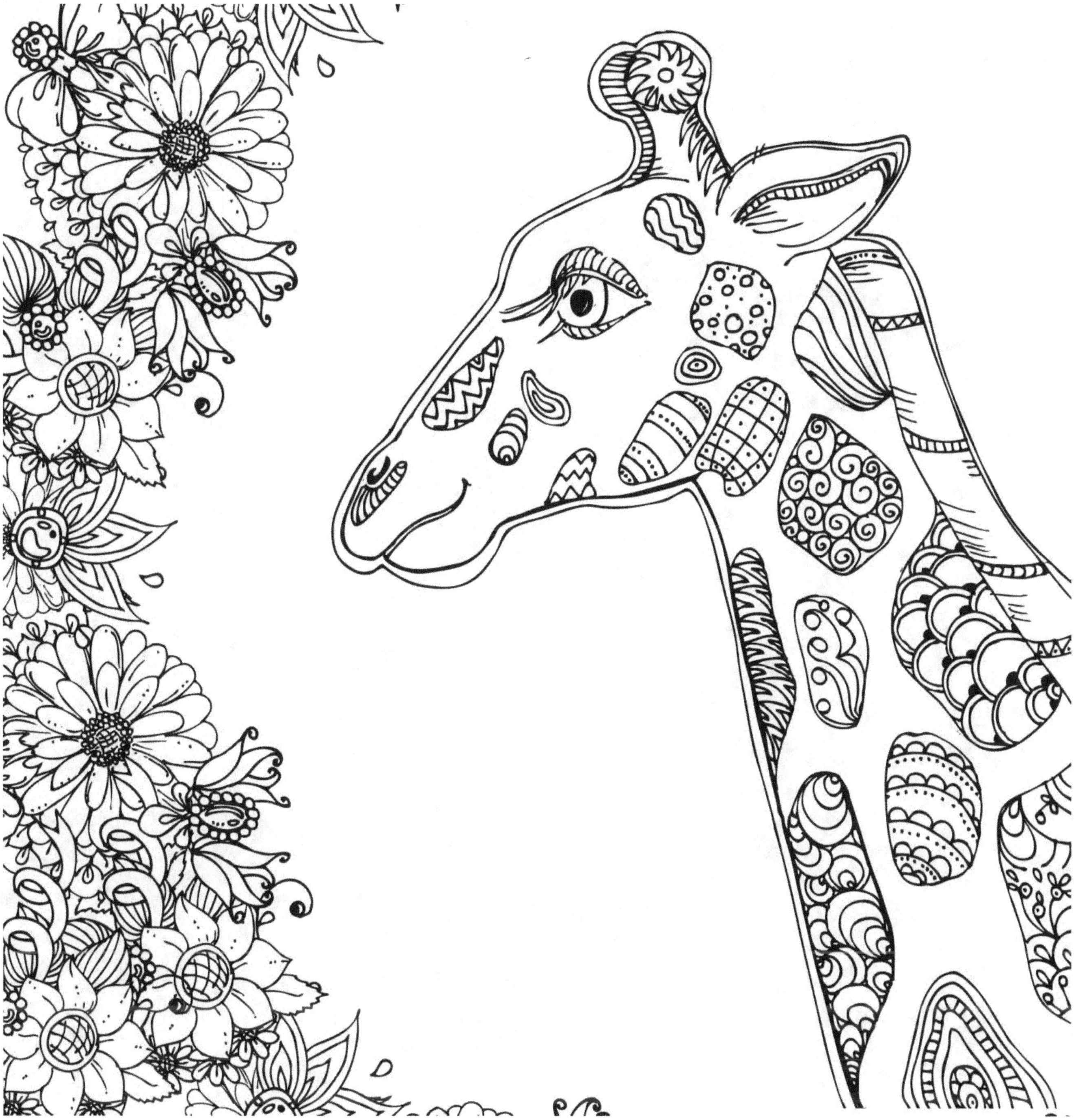

www.ingramcontent.com/pod-product-compliance
Lightning Source LLC
Chambersburg PA
CBHW081132180526
45170CB00008B/3079